Bluffer's Guides

CENTENNIAL PRESS

MW01016507

THE VALLEY

• G

F

MOUNTAINS

• E

• H

A

• D HOLLYWOOD

C

N

B

• WEST HOLLYWOOD

M

• I

K

DOWNTOWN
LA.

L

• J

GREATER
LOS ANGELES

A. MALIBU
B. GETTY
   MUSEUM
C. BEL AIR
D. BEVERLY
   HILLS
E. HOLLYWOOD
   BOWL
F. UNIVERSAL
   STUDIOS
G. BURBANK

H. FOREST LAWN
I. FOX
J. MGM
K. SANTA MONICA
L. VENICE
M. BRENTWOOD
N. PASADENA
   Rose Bowl
   Huntington Library

BLUFF YOUR WAY IN HOLLYWOOD

Virginia J. Nelson
Colin Clements

CENTENNIAL PRESS

ISBN 0-8220-2207-9
U.S. edition © Copyright 1989 by Centennial Press
British edition © Copyright 1987 by The Bluffer's Guides

Printed in U.S.A.
All Rights Reserved

Centennial Press, Box 82087, Lincoln, Nebraska 68501
an imprint of Cliffs Notes, Inc.

INTRODUCTION

Hooray for *Hollywood!* . . . the bluffer's paradise! A town where having tons of money, knowing the right people, and being dazzling of smile and hard of body are undeniable advantages, but are *not* essential. This is Tinseltown, where the stuff of Make Believe is Where It's At. Nowhere else in America (outside of national politics and high stakes Vegas-style poker) can so much (money) be made with so little (talent). One must, however, know how to speak the language in order to gain a toehold in the slippery scramble for those visible symbols of success that are of infinite importance in wonderful, wonderous Hollywood.

To begin with, Hollywood is the moviemaking capital of the world. *Wro-o-o-nng!* Behind Hollywood's facade, you'll discover that the place itself is 100% manufactured myth. "Hollywood," the actual *town* of Hollywood, is a sleazy, rundown section of northwestern Los Angeles. Motel rooms are available by the hour, the cuisine is a grim array of fast food—and smack dab in the middle of everything is Frederick's of Hollywood, the firm that publishes that soft-porn catalogue of fantasy lingerie that pre-pubescent boys and old men drool and dribble over.

On the brighter side, though, Hollywood Boulevard still boasts Mann's (formerly Grauman's) Chinese Theater, the pagoda-style extravaganza of a movie house, whose cement entryway still features the hand,

3

foot, breast (and occasional hoof and paw) prints of Hollywood stars. And yes, the sidewalks are still embedded with brass stars honoring various achievements in the entertainment industry. And it's also true that the landmark **HOLLYWOOD** sign still overlooks the urban sprawl from its hillside, proclaiming the Hollywood legend in letters forty feet high.

But, where Chaplin, Pickford, Garbo, and Gable once trod, there's now only *one* major movie studio in operation, Paramount. Columbia nearly went down the tubes over a dozen years ago and had to sell their studio to pay off their debts; the Goldwyn studio still functions (well, kind of; for several years, it was an anyone-can-rent-it facility). Recently, it's ventured back into production status, but the studio retains little of the glamour associated with its movie mogul origins. And the other big movie studios are scattered throughout the Los Angeles area (which is a *lot* of area)–miles from Hollywood proper. This doesn't make any real difference–except to tourists, who are always upset to learn that stars and starlets and movie moguls don't actually live in Hollywood any more. Today's male Hollywood stars are usually tucked away in shoreline "cottages," luxurious apartments, hi-tech haciendas, and opulent hotels and palatial estates from Malibu to Mulholland Drive and from Broad Beach to Beverly Hills and as far from Hollywood as possible: Clint Eastwood lives in Carmel, Burt Reynolds in Florida, Paul Newman in Connecticut, Robert Redford in Utah, and Marlon Brando on his own South Sea island. On the other hand, famous female stars are usually found at fat farms (sweating it out), at Betty Ford's (drying

4

out), or in a plastic surgeon's operation room (having it carved out).

However, all this isn't what Hollywood is *really* all about. Hollywood is about Glitz and Glamour, Big Deals over Power Lunches, High Visibility, and Hot Properties. In short, Hollywood is a dream come true for the bluffer. Not so much a place – as a state of mind.

WELCOME TO L.A.

"L.A.," the "City of Angels," the "Big Orange" or, simply, "the Coast." All of these names refer to "Greater Los Angeles," that big chunk of southern California that includes all of the area within the Los Angeles basin, along with 11 million people, 4½ million cars, and 6,500 miles of freeway and surface streets. Its location on a coastal plain between the Pacific Ocean and the Santa Monica Mountains ensures a predictably year-round mild climate – mild, that is, except for the toxic, yellow-orange exhaust fumes of an ever-increasing number of vehicles traveling this labyrinth of roadways, combined with industrial pollution and the evaporation of thousands of chemically treated swimming pools. All of which spells S-M-O-G.

Smog is particularly heavy in the summer and early autumn, but it's particularly allergy-rich and in abundance *every day*. All-pervasive and ever-present, it's pushed inland by the ocean breezes and trapped by the Hollywood Hills, creating a coagulated aura that's distinctive and deadly – an aura that's – well, Hollywood.

Anyone flying into Los Angeles will fly into LAX (pronounced "el-ay-ex" – and not "lax," a word which would immediately expose you as unknowing and hopelessly un-hip). From the air, you won't see much of the city – except for upward reflections from the city's glittering, blue-painted pools and its vast net-

6

works of freeways, barely visible through the haze. But you'll see the orange smog.

The peculiarly "orange" color of the smog is one of the reasons for L.A.'s nickname—the Big Orange. The local Chamber of Commerce would like folks from out of town to think that the name is a clever historical nod, since the area was once covered with orange groves. Give the Chamber of Commerce boys an F for fourth-rate bluffing. The notion of a large-metropolitan-area-as-fruit (New York being the Big Apple) just doesn't cut it in L.A. When was the last time that you heard Richard Dreyfus refer to his hometown as the Big Orange?

If you want to be perceived as a knowledgeable native, don't mention the Big Orange or even say "Los Angeles." *Always* say "L.A." And if you're talking about the *greater* Los Angeles area while you're in New York (referred to in L.A. as "the City"), you should refer to L.A. as "the Coast" (this is particularly effective if shouted into a telephone in a major hotel lobby, as in "Get me 'the Coast'!"). Clearly, L.A. requires a little further explanation.

L.A. is a city of contrasts. We're talking about a 60-mile-wide suburb that covers a multitude of sins—literally as well as figuratively. Homes range from Ron and Nancy Reagan's $2.5 million "bungalow" in Bel-Air to the tract houses of East L.A. And we're also talking businesses; L.A. has everything from oil wells to shopping malls, theme parks to factories. There's something for everyone in L.A.

Los Angeles is indisputably materialistic and shallow—the deepest things being the Jacuzzis. It's also ridiculously expensive ($4.00 for a glass of Perrier) and hot and smoggy (smog alerts are continuously broadcast on TV and radio, advising people with bronchial problems to stay indoors). In addition, it's ridiculously lacking in original theater and literature. Everyone, it seems, is always "working on" a screenplay, but this is *not* to be confused with writing literature. Even the local newspaper, the *Los Angeles Times* has a less-than-stellar reputation. Woody Allen once claimed that L.A.'s sole contribution to civilization is the right to turn right on red. He's right.

What, then, makes L.A. so appealing? That's easy. The glamour and the excitement, the sunshine and the beaches. The chance to make it BIG – sell that script, be discovered, rub shoulders with the Rich and Famous, have seats for Lakers' games, or get a personal "hello" from the owner of Ma Maison. And, if you're satisfied with seeing merely the "trappings" of success, L.A.'s the place for you: it's got bus tours of stars' homes, unlimited gawking at awards ceremony entrances, and there's always a chance that you'll spot a real, live Star in a local restaurant. So, welcome to L.A.! Your Bluffer's Guide in hand, look beyond the tinsel and see the *real* tinsel.

The Hollywood Sign

Disappointed starlets have leapt to their death from it. Like a gigantic vanity plate on a custom car, it stands for anything that you want to believe about Hollywood. The original purpose of the imposing letters (50 feet high, 30 feet wide) on the south side of Mt. Lee in the Hollywood Hills was not to make the movie capital visible from airplanes, or provide a springboard for less-than-successful actresses, or even to make available one of the best location-establishing shots for the film industry. No, the sign which originally read "HOLLYWOOD*LAND*" was constructed in 1923 to advertise a cute little subdivision in nearby Beachwood Canyon – all winding streets, red tiles, stucco and azaleas – where movie moguls maintained love nests and where discreet murders were committed in Raymond Chandler's mystery novels. In the late 40s, the Hollywood Chamber of Commerce removed the "LAND" from the sign. Then in the late 70s, the sign began looking pretty grim. The letters were leaning or were missing altogether, the paint was peeling, and the undergirding structure was beginning to crumble. Fortunately, in a flurry of generous affection generally reserved for charity dinners, celebrity roasts, and funerals for past Oscar winners, Hollywood stars (like Alice Cooper, Gene Autry, and Andy Williams, for example; civic spirit makes strange bedfellows) donated money for a new sign, at a cost of 27K per letter. By the end of '78, the sign had been re-created in weather-resistant steel and concrete, and once again, all was well with the world. One does wonder, however, what all of those disappointed, suicide-prone starlets did in the meantime – bided their time in aerobics classes?

The lesson for the bluffer is this: hype has a permanent home in Hollywood. Legends are far more durable than reality.

GETTING AROUND

"L.A. is a great big freeway . . ."; so goes the Burt Bacharach song (Burt had obviously spent some real time behind the wheel in L.A.). When heading for Hollywood, one follows the great golden swathe (read *smog*) of Los Angeles that lies between the foothills and canyons of the Santa Monica Mountains, from slightly north of Sunset, through "the Flats," to a few blocks below Wilshire, and continues west from Hollywood itself through West Hollywood, Beverly Hills, Westwood, Brentwood, Bel-Air, and Pacific Palisades to West Malibu, Broad Beach, and Trancas. Got it?

The majority of these towns are separate municipalities, so in addition to having their own distinct personalities, they have their own police forces – that is, LAPD (the Los Angeles Police Department, featured in Joseph Wambaugh's novels) patrols the streets of L.A. proper, but a *town* like Beverly Hills has its *own* police department. This wasn't originally intended as a way of providing seemingly endless material for Eddie Murphy movies; it just seems that way. And the *county* of Los Angeles is served by yet another organization, policed by a sheriff. And the *state* of California is policed by the California Highway Patrol, or CHiPs. Here, the dramatic potential of snappy, tight 'n trim uniforms and mirrored sunglasses on a couple of hunky guys proved too great to be overlooked. *CHiPs* became a popular TV show in the 70s. Hollywood never tires of Art imitating Life.

It's of utmost importance for the bluffer to distinguish between where one *is* and where one *wants to be* in L.A. (in general) and in Hollywood (in particular). The operative word here is "arriving," and the astute bluffer will automatically place more emphasis on the time spent in more desirable areas. Although every region has its points, here's some highlights for the aspiring bluffer.

West Hollywood

Located between Hollywood and Beverly Hills, West Hollywood has the distinction of being the first officially gay city in the United States. This may or may not be the reason for the preponderance of fashionable restaurants and ultra-chic interior designer shops (located on Robertson Boulevard and known as Designers Row). Purportedly, the town boasts more dry cleaners per square mile than anywhere else in the world. What *that* means is anybody's guess. This stretch of Melrose Avenue (one of the major East-West thoroughfares) is usually referred to as the "Soho of Southern California" because of the profusion of galleries, cafes, boutiques, and specialty stories that have sprung up in the last ten years. Not as pricey as Rodeo Drive, the businesses here reflect the newest trends and a flamboyance not found anywhere else in L.A.

Beverly Hills

Robert Redford once observed that "if you stay in Beverly Hills too long you turn into a Mercedes." Probably true. Beverly Hills is reputedly the richest city per capita in the world, where the chic meet the shieks. It's a town stuffed with Really Big Money, much of it generated by "the Industry" (a handy catch-all term for any business even *remotely* connected to moviemaking; for example, an astute bluffer would refer to his job of delivering pizzas to a movie set as "time spent working in 'the Industry'").

Beverly Hills is the apex of the American Dream, the circus tent of status and success, the cornucopia of conspicuous consumption. And lest you think that we exaggerate, let us give you examples: the mansions in L.A. are indeed *fabulous*, the lawns (in an area where water is money) are *all* lush and green and manicured, and beyond the city's commercial center, the only sounds one hears are the occasional chirp of a well-mannered robin or two and the low hum of expensive cars – Rolls Royces and, of course, *Mercedes*. It's illegal to honk your horn in Beverly Hills after business hours, and although it's *not* illegal to walk there, it *does* look suspicious. When Dino de Laurentiis first moved to Beverly Hills in the 70s, he thought he would get a little early morning exercise by walking the few blocks from his mansion to his executive offices. Halfway there, he was picked up by a Beverly Hills cop for interrogation and had to be rescued by his chauffeur, who was following a discreet block and a half behind him.

Shopping is the optimal activity in Beverly Hills because it gives you three simultaneous opportunities for showing off your wealth – arriving in an expensive custom car, wearing expensive custom clothes, and spending ridiculous amounts of money on things you absolutely *don't* need. Bluffers, take note. In Beverly Hills, Appearance Is Reality. Some stores here are *so* exclusive and *so* pricey that the likes of Gucci, Cartier, and Ralph Lauren seem positively pedestrian by comparison.

Bijan on Rodeo Drive is perhaps Beverly Hills' *most* exclusive shop. We're talking "by invitation only." It's a place so smart that it refuses even to refer to itself as a shop. It calls itself a "designer showroom." Suits retail for around two thousand apiece; a tie goes for an H-buck, and a mink-lined jacket costs more than most cars. This is sacred ground for serious shoppers.

Down the block is Kazanjian Brothers. At least $6 million worth of trinkets are usually on display and another $30 million in the vault. Jeweler Ron Kazanjian co-produced (appropriately enough) the smash hit *Romancing the Stone.* Not only do the rich get richer in Hollywood—they get a *lot* richer.

Giorgio's, popularized in the Judith Krantz novel *Scruples*, is almost in the same league as Bijan. One doesn't need an appointment, but the surroundings are almost as posh. It has a clublike atmosphere, where the well-heeled can play billiards or enjoy an expresso or cocktail (gratis, naturally) while selecting from an abundance of beautiful men's and women's clothing. To save his pampered customers the inconvenience of toting packages home, Giorgio's sends them to your home or hotel in a classic Rolls Royce. A thoughtful gesture.

The Price of His Toys store seemingly operates from the theory that "if it's practical or a necessity, we don't stock it." Here is, at last, the spot we've all dreamed about—the place to pick up those $200 pogo sticks and those $1000 air pistols for those hard-to-buy-for friends and business acquaintances. And for that really special someone, a solar-powered model train that fits into an attache case (a mere $2800).

Do kids figure into your shopping list? Worry no more. Rodeo Coach, specializing in RRs, Lamborghinis, and Ferraris, has cars for kiddies. Take your platinum charge card, though. Powered with a 3-horse engine and zooming along at 30 mph, they retail *way* above the budget of even the most zealously upward-oriented middle-class wannabe.

Time out. It's truly hard to bluff Big Bucks. Let's head out beyond the green-backed, rarified air of Beverly Hills, towards Westwood. Westwood is home to UCLA. It's also home to a number of movie theaters that function as "proving grounds." Films are often trotted out here to see if the public likes them. Usually, they're sent back to the editors for fine-tuning. As a result, more than one happy ending has been tacked onto a grimly realistic movie in hopes of boosting its audience appeal.

Brentwood, Bel-Air, and Pacific Palisades are all sleekly rustic – very fashionable and expensive sub-urbs – and as you pass through them, be aware that you're heading toward the beach and – finally – fresh, clear air.

Before we get there, though, we hit Santa Monica, an autonomous town. It's on the much-heralded "Coast." George Lucas and Stephen Spielberg keep their production offices here. The tone is understated and quiet. This is an acceptable address and has one enviable asset: a fairly dependable supply of quality oxygen.

South of Santa Monica is Venice, famous for its boardwalk that's always awash with bicyclists, roller skaters, break dancers, and the gawkers they attract.

It's also the home of Muscle Beach, where aspiring Arnold Schwarzeneggers pump up their pecs and pose. Venice lacks class, but it more than makes up for it with charm. Gregory Hines hung out here before his recent climb to the top.

To the north, on the Pacific Coast Highway, lie the Beach Colonies. The most famous is Malibu, but Broad Beach (farther north) is newer and more exclusive. Goldie Hawn and Walter Matthau have (or had) the kind of homes here that regularly make the pages of *Architectural Digest*. Trancas, even farther north, is growing in status, but it's a bit of a drive. The Colonies are the weekend unwinding playgrounds for the Rich and Famous, and, as such, they have an abundance of Star-gazing opportunities. The beaches are private (in theory), but you can gain access easily by simply acting like you belong there. You'd probably want to take this a step further and make up a fictitious excuse — say that you're visting your "close personal friend Bruce Willis." Take care, though, not to venture *too* near his home.

Basically, the Colonies are studies in being Laid Back (California-speak for "relaxed"). The only thing that causes the local pulses to quicken are the not-infrequent, property-endangering, act-of-God disasters — mud slides, earthquakes, brush fires, and high tides that can instantly turn expensive real estate into so much flotsam. But few Colonists would ever think of moving out (except to make a killing on their property). A solid, warm camaraderie exists among the stalwarts who live here. Once during a storm-lashed dinner party in Malibu, it was learned that one of the neighbors had just lost his guest house.

"Anybody in it?" someone asked.
"Nobody bankable," someone else answered back.
So much for beach bitchiness. Back to L.A.

L.A. is peculiar because it has no real *center*. It has a downtown, containing City Hall, the main police station, some federal buildings and skyscrapers, a Chinatown, Little Tokyo, Skid Row, an architecturally stunning 30s Deco railroad station, and really grand hotels (the spectacularly modern Bonaventure, as well as the newly refurbished "Toast of the Coast," the Biltmore). Unfortunately, however, L.A.'s downtown is *not* the center of *any*thing. It's miles from anywhere – about 20 miles from Hollywood. And it's only in the last couple of years that young artists and designers started converting the old warehouses of L.A. proper into studios and lofts; sharp realtors followed in their wake. Inevitably, the gentrification process will begin.

The Valley

North of the hills lies the San Fernando Valley, home of Universal Studios. Also out here is beautiful downtown Burbank, home of NBC and the butt of many a Johnny Carson joke. Also in the foothills is Studio City, the dormitory of ambitious young studio execs. Bluffers, be advised – these are Fringe Areas.

Beyond this, there's sort of a colonized desert – a flat, endless, hot and smoggy suburb in a frying pan. Worse than the geography, however, are the inhabitants: a collection of fourth assistant directors, snake handlers, failed writers, best boys, key grips, and other people whose names roll up in the movie credits long after everyone has filed out of a movie theater. Some of them claim to "really like" the Valley, swearing that it's a piece of genuine Americana. No doubt these same people, if they had only one day to spend in New Orleans, would opt to take a 4-hour guided tour of the swamps.

THE HOLLYWOOD DREAM

Lana Turner was plucked out of obscurity at Schwab's Drugstore (now Schwab's Pharmacy) on Sunset Boulevard, featured in a movie, and, as the "sweater girl," became an overnight sensation. Or so goes the apochryphal story, which is handed down as genuine Hollywood lore. And one should *never* argue; Hollywood believes these rags-to-riches stories. Hollywood believes in the depths of its soul that Dreams Can Come True—that Somebody Up There Likes You, that the Force can be with you and that miracles *can* really happen. This is why so many Hollywood movies have happy endings—why Rocky becomes world champion and why E.T. gets to phone home. This is why, every year, thousands of young hopefuls flood into L.A. and wait tables, park cars, go to acting classes, flock to cattle-call auditions, and continue to believe that they're going to become one of the Chosen, one of the ones who Make It, *the* one who becomes a S*T*A*R.

And it isn't only actors and actresses who have these dreams. The kid in the mailroom and the gofer on the set believe it too. So do screenwriters, directors, agents, producers, *and* studio executives. They're all infected by the same dream and by the same intoxicating hope: Someday, they'll become rich, famous, and successful—someday, they'll be *Somebody*.

It's possible. Some of the greatest movie moguls didn't

start out in the movie business. They began their careers selling gloves, hauling junk, plugging songs, and mending shoes. Men like . . .

Louis B. Mayer

A former scrap metal dealer; under his forceful (some say dictatorial) control, MGM became the unquestioned industry leader, having a galaxy of stars under contract ("More stars than there are in heaven," according to studio publicists).

Adolph Zukor

A former nickelodeon owner and Hungarian immigrant, he emerged from a series of mergers to head Paramount; he finally expired at the age of 103.

The Warner Brothers

The former exhibitors—Albert, Harry M., Sam, and the youngest and most famous, Jack—were indeed all brothers. (Jack reputedly ran the studio like a prison warden.)

Harry Cohn

A former song plugger and vaudevillian, he built Columbia from the profits he made selling a picture called *Traffic in Souls*. (If Louis B. Mayer was a dictator, Harry "King" Cohn was an absolute monster.)

Darryl F. Zanuck

From Wahoo, Nebraska (a real town), he started his film career writing stories for Rin Tin Tin and worked his way up to being a producer at Warners before taking over at Twentieth-Century Fox. He was famous for his wraparound sunglasses, big cigars, and the injunction "Don't say 'Yes' until I finish talking." As an independent, he produced the blockbuster *Longest Day*. He was, in a very real sense, the Last Tycoon.

Add to this list the more recent success stories of George Lucas and Lawrence Kasden, and you can see why every new hopeful who arrives in Hollywood firmly believes, "If *they* can make it, why not *me*?"

THE HOLLYWOOD
SOCIAL SCENE

In Hollywood, everything depends on which way you're going – upwards, downwards, or standing still. There's nothing Hollywood fears as much as failure – or even the *smell* of it. People will glad-hand you and say "Hi" in the commissary once you've begun your climb upwards, but if anyone begins a whispering campaign about your starting *downwards*, your phone automatically stops ringing. Failure is looked upon as a communicable disease. You become Untouchable.

Clearly, Hollywood is a highly snobbish, class- and caste-conscious town. There are, for instance, the A, B, and C social lists. The A-list includes people like studio heads, top agents, heavyweight producers and directors and, of course, Stars. Such luminaries *rarely* mingle with the lower orders (like bit players or technicians; a possible exception is Burt Reynolds, who loves to hang around with stuntmen). Most of the older, legendary stars are on the A-list. This is the closest thing to royalty in America. These are the folks who receive Lifetime Achievement Awards at Oscar time. The whole crowd gets to their feet and applauds for five minutes.

Believe it not, the applause is real. It's a genuine outpouring of emotion – awe and respect for talent and professional longevity. Those who are applauding know what an accomplishment it is to have hung on in the highly precarious, dog-eat-dog world of show biz. Each person applauding is sending up a prayer that they too will have that kind of immortality in a town without a heart, where success and failure rest on the caprice of the notoriously fickle public. Lasting stardom must be established over the Long Haul in order to have value. The currently popular box office phenoms like Tom Cruise, Tom Hanks, and Michael J. Fox may be "bankable," but they're far from being eligible for the A-lists.

Age and Staying Power, however, aren't the only criteria for inclusion on the A-list. There's also Style. However hot Madonna or one of Martin Sheen's kids currently is, they're not, socially speaking, A-list material. Top Hollywood parties – as opposed to general bashes like premiere parties or post-Oscar get-togethers – tend to be cast as carefully as *Gone with the Wind*. Let's face it, would you seat Sylvester Stallone next to Katherine Hepburn? Sean Penn next to anyone?

The people who attend A-list parties are the people who *give* A-list parties; it's an incestuous little round dance if ever there was one. But even at this exalted level, the most inveterate partygivers are those who can claim them as tax deductions or, better yet, get the studio to pay for them.

The town's best partygivers are agents Swifty Lazar and Sue Mengers, ex-agent and production chief Barry Diller, and MCA's boss, Lew Wasserman. Obviously, for them, "packaging" – putting together an irresistible combination of talent and anticipation – is so much a part of their business that it extends to guest lists and catering. This transforms these little *fetes* into stunning tributes to sensory stimulation – beautiful food, flowers, and people against a backdrop of stunning homes. In short, true Hollywood.

The sole limitation of agents' parties is that, other than "neutral guests" (studio heads and independent producers), their guest list is pretty much limited to their agency's clients. Of course, discreet poaching of Hot Properties (in this case, actors) goes on all the time. In fact, a new acquisition by an agent usually calls for a party.

Studio execs, producers, directors, actors, and so on, don't have this limitation and can invite anyone they like, although if you're the head of Columbia, you're unlikely to invite the head of Fox. It's also probably unwise to bring together two heavyweight producers. In contrast, directors, actors, and writers all share a professional camaraderie which, however thin the veneer, can be counted on to keep the proceedings civil. Producers, however, are of another ilk. They're the movie industry's lone wolves. Of all the Hollywood players, they're more self-reliant, more competitive, and more hard-assed—meaning, they bluff better than any of the rest.

One case in point is a legend in Tinseltown. Dino de Laurentiis and Jon Peters (ex-hairdresser and, at that time, Barbra Streisand's lover and producer) found themselves at the same party. Both had pictures just released—Dino had *King Kong* and Peters had *A Star Is Born*. Not renowned for his tact, Peters bragged that his film was out-grossing Dino's. Dino eyed him coldly and snapped back, "Yeah, but your monkey sings!"

Despite all of the reputed hoopla, however, Hollywood has never been a late-night town. Top movie parties break up early because a day's shooting gears

25

up in the pre-dawn hours, and even if you're not working, you want to *pretend* that you are. Even the desk-bound paper-pushers and deal-makers have their 7 A.M. tennis games, after which it's becoming increasingly fashionable to have a session with one's "personal trainer." The late Bebe Daniels once remarked that the invention of sound ruined Hollywood as a party town: "Instead of playing around at night, you have to go home and learn your damn lines!"

Most of the late-night revelers in recent years have been members of the music crowd, and because of their all-night recording sessions, they've always kept odd hours. As the art crowd grows in popularity and number, a decidedly New York influence is creeping into Hollywood. Dancing—whether it's Slam, Disco, or Vogueing—is again becoming popular at clubs like the Whiskey and Nucleus Nuance on Melrose, where one can dance and eat until two in the morning.

It's a decided risk to publicly ask anyone about their "spouse" in Hollywood. Working on projects in close proximity for months at a time—often far from home—makes for coupling standards somewhat more liberal than they are, say, in Hominy, Oklahoma. California is a community property state—meaning that, in the event of a divorce, *all* possessions (kids, pets, homes, cash, post-Impressionist paintings, etc.) get split 50/50 by husband and wife. And nowadays, couples don't even have to be married—or be of two different sexes—to claim entitlement to alimony, or in non-marriage affiliations, "palimony." This can be a touchy subject with some people. The wise bluffer will comment on the smog.

Some people in Hollywood, however, are actually

famous for the number of times that they've been up the aisle. It's an accepted method of raising one's social status (and sometimes one's income). Zsa Zsa Gabor was just married for the eighth time (dahlink) to the man who runs Consolidated Oil and owns half of downtown. Liz Taylor has been quiet for a while, but has tied the knot more than half a dozen times. Mickey Rooney has been married eight times and managed to stay friends with his bank manager throughout, a remarkable occurrence considering the amount of alimony he must pay.

This isn't exactly a new phenomenon either. Years ago, Will Rogers quipped, "I'm not really a movie star—I still got the same wife I started out with 28 years ago." But there *are* happy marriages in Hollywood, just as there's long-standing love affairs (of the Tracy-Hepburn variety), and knowing who is committedly sleeping with whom can be instrumental in getting a project off the ground.

For instance, Blake Edwards (director of *The Pink Panther* and *Victor/Victoria*) is married to Julie Andrews. Find a classy comedy script that she can star in and one which he can direct—and you've got the makings of a "package." The same can be said of Sam Shepard and Jessica Lange. *Prizzi's Honor* went even one better by bringing together a then long-standing Item—Jack Nicholson and Angelica Huston—as well as her father, the late actor/director John Huston. And there's historical precedent: Burton and Taylor, Bogie and Bacall, Gable and Lombard, Garbo and Gilbert, Fairbanks and Pickford, McQueen and McGraw, and Mickey and Minnie.

If you still aren't convinced that love and money go

cheek-to-jowl in Hollywood, bear in mind that the common parlance for "cutting a deal" is "getting into bed" with someone. At least once, try to sound like a studio exec—just for the chance to say that you're "getting into bed with Mel Gibson" or "getting into bed with Kathleen Turner," if only in the figurative sense.

Sex, Drugs, and Rock and Roll

Sex

It's not surprising in a town where so much time and energy (not to mention cold cash) go into making people attractive (to directors, agents, and, certainly, the public) that libido runs in high gear. Southern California has long been known for for its easy, relaxed attitude, and this certainly extends into matters sexual. Hollywood movies are, in one sense, a reflection of the mores of America. But it's also an accepted fact that the people who make these movies are not only allowed—but even expected—to live lives of exotic passion and flamboyant hedonism. Recently, however, the threat of contracting a fatal disease has thrown a wrench into Hollywood's swinging lifestyle. Soap opera stars are demanding "no kiss" clauses in their contracts, Hugh Hefner is rumored to be selling off the Playboy mansion, and even the term "orgy" seems like a humorous relic of the 70s, gone the way of gold neckchains and platform shoes.

Still, nature and opportunity being what they are, casting couches remain a time-honored part of Hollywood folklore and "servicing the producer" and "working your way to the top on your back" are still part of the game. The only difference today is that more producers and more major players are *women*, and some of them have been known to take just as much advantage of their position as their male counterparts. This has given rise to the "toy boys," the male equivalent of the empty-headed, attractive starlets, more popular for their performances *off*screen.

Drugs

Convinced that L.A. is Hip City, wide-eyed Midwesterners arrive convinced that possession of marijuana is O.K. — as long as there's not too much of it and it's for "personal, recreational use" and not for sale. It isn't so. You'll probably get busted faster in L.A. than in Des Moines. And as for cocaine — bluffers, beware. As Richard Pryor (whose drug exploits are almost legendary) has said, "Cocaine is God's way of telling you that you have too much money." *However* (and this "however" rarely applies to bluffers), if you're sufficiently affluent and have the right connections, you can have drugs delivered like pizzas.

In the 60s and 70s, even studio heads who wanted to be trendy were not adverse to an occasional puff or snort. But times have changed. People on A-lists rarely indulge anymore and often take part in national campaigns to steer young people away from drugs and alcohol. In fact, it's become far more fashionable to be a Betty Ford Clinic graduate, which has the twin advantages of sobering you up and at the same time generating a lot of media attention. All of the really Hot Properties these days are "just saying No," as Nancy Reagan advised. Rarely do people go scooting off to the bathroom for a quick toot. Designer water bars and

Friday night meetings of Alcoholics Anonymous have become the new "places to been seen in." Even cigarette smoking, the very thing that launched the careers of Joan Bennett and Bette Davis, is often looked down on with a certain self-righteous disdain.

Rock and Roll

Hollywood is one of the great pop-rock recording centers of the world, home of the prolific Lionel Ritchie, the Eagles (who captured the essence of southern California perfectly with such songs as "Life in the Fast Lane" and "Hotel California"), and, more recently, girl groups like the Bangles. Until the last few years, the movie scene and the music scene rarely overlapped – if for no other reason than they keep different hours. However, starting with *Flashdance* in the early 80s, it became abundantly clear just how lucrative the marriage of popular music and film could be. Since then, more projects are in the works, capitalizing on crossover talents and sure sales.

Bodyworks

Hollywood and L.A. are much more obsessed by Beautiful People than, say, New York. The most obvious reason is that the weather in California is conducive to fewer clothes and more swimming pools.

The degree of narcissism displayed in Hollywood is staggering. Fifty-year-old-plus studio executives risk coronary by-pass surgery by playing daily sets of tennis. In a town that reveres youth and health, they swig Perrier and munch so-called wholefoods (lots of natural fiber) and punish themselves with aerobics. The streets

30

teem with joggers, Walkmans plugged in their ears, running the risk of not hearing sleek, ubiquitous cars and becoming a fashionable grease spot in their Lycra bodysuits.

Hollywood joggers wear the most aerodynamically sound running shoes available and special watches that digitize their heart rate, blood sugar, and even show how many calories have been burned. It doesn't seem to occur to these "fit people" that inhaling smog at an increased rate is like spending half an hour's time hyperventilating in an elevator full of cigar smokers. In contrast, cyclists in L.A. tend to be smarter. They wear smog masks.

Other fashionable attempts to keep in shape include pumping iron. Once considered to be the exclusive domain of hollow-headed hunks at Muscle Beach, lifting free weights and working out on Nautilus-type equipment is not only acceptable today, but encouraged for men *and* women.

Who can argue with Cher when she says in the Vic Tanney ad, "If a body like this came in a bottle, everyone would have one." Arnold Schwarzenegger made the successful transition from world-class muscleman to box office gold and even went one better by marrying into the Kennedy family. It's enough to make anyone do a few sit-ups.

To keep their current Hot Properties in shape, studios and agents often have not only a trainer for their stable of actors but also a nutritionist. *Every*thing shows up on the screen, and in this town, unless one wants to become strictly a character actor, what shows up should look *healthy*.

Despite the preponderance of swimming pools,

swimming is *not* a particularly popular form of exercise in Hollywood. "Swimming" is left to the kids at Laguna Beach. "Pools," on the other hand, function as yet one more visible symbol of wealth. They're the preferred places to "take a meeting" (or a phone call) at the fashionable hotels. Pools also are an indispensable part of Hollywood, because they provide the impetus for female stars to show up in swimming suits. Marilyn Monroe, Deborah Kerr, Ursula Andress, Bo Derek, Esther Williams, and Annette Funicello are all a part of this time-honored tradition.

For those who have tried all of the exercises and oats and mineral waters and still suffer sags and bags, bulges and baldness, take heart. In Hollywood, an entire industry has sprung up in order to eliminate such unsightly problems.

Dentistry

Even mere mortals outside La-La Land (yet another moniker for L.A.) value a beautiful smile that flashes even, white teeth. But in the land of the Close-up, this is a *necessity*. This is why "cosmetic dentistry" is such a booming business and includes not only root canals, bridge work, capping, and crowning, but also whitening and ceramic bonding—all to provide a dazzling All-American Hollywood Smile.

Hair Replacement

Baldness in Hollywood is referred to with a somewhat gentler term: "hair loss." Even so, the term can be deadly to a man's commercial sex appeal. If you're Sean Connery, Frank Sinatra, or Burt Reynolds, you can get away with wearing a toupee ("rug"), often-

times at studio expense. Others try everything from twining what's left into long strands and, using creative parting techniques, attempting to disguise the devastation. This doesn't play well in Peoria – or in Hollywood. Others have been driven to smearing their scalps with yak's urine. The trendy solutions today are hair weaving (combining the hair you have left with other – sometimes natural, sometimes not – stringy tufts to thicken the overall appearance) and transplanting (taking skin and hair follicles from other, hairier parts of your anatomy and surgically securing or plugging them into your scalp). Of course, there's always *hats* (Paul Anka, teen singing idol of the 60s and creator of Sinatra's signature song, "I Did It My Way," has been a hat man for years, as, of course, has Sinatra himself).

Plastic Surgery

Here's *true* Hollywood at its most creative best – anatomical artistry offering a whole menu of surgical alterations for every part of the body you can think of – abdominoplasty, liposuction, buttock lifts, rhinoplasty (a nose job), breast enlargements (Mariel Hemingway's for *Star 80*), chemabrasion, and, yes, silicone *lip* enlargements (Barbara Hersey). The list is endless. If you can remodel your mansion, why not remodel your whatever(s)? Even if your smile becomes (dare we say, like Phyllis Diller's) a little "fixed" and rumors abound that it's possible to strike matches on your forehead – hey, if it takes a few years off the chassis, why not? In Phyllis's case, it's rumored there were enough parts left over after her multiple operations to build a whole new star.

All of this vanity is buttressed by a more-than-generous selection of beauty parlors, hair and skin-care salons, nail-care boutiques, and tanning joints (for those who can't seem to make it to the beach, in a town on the ocean, where the sun shines 360 days a year). There's also a whole range of dietary and cosmetic products — from all-natural to high-tech. Remember that in Hollywood, the term "make-up" is something that's worn when "making movies." When you're shopping, you're shopping for "cosmetics" or "health and beauty aids." Here, as in so many areas of Hollywood life, what you *call* a thing is every bit as important as what it actually *is*.

If all else fails — the porcelain bonding, the pool-proof hair, and the liposucked buttocks — and you find yourself panting for popularity or stardom but running out of body parts to overhaul, take heart. There's always the "inner you."

In Hollywood, there's no shortage of psychotherapists, counselors, and self-improvement programs like Rolfing (backrubs practiced in Hell), est (anywhere but in California you'd get backhanded for letting loose with a primal scream), churches (*nothing* like the foot-washing Baptists ever envisioned), and more eccentric cults than you can shake a stick at. In Hollywood, these are legitimate places for "networking." Having a spiritual reader or channeler in common is terrific common ground for "cutting a deal."

The last resort for absolute preservation of that great body and dental work is, of course, embalming. But bear in mind that even here, there's places where one should *not* be caught dead. The Hollywood Cemetery, which had two thousand mourners when Valentino died, is fashionable no more. Unless you plan on leaving instructions for your ashes to be scattered over some fashionable watering hole, the only place to be planted for eternity is Forest Lawn. *Mirabile Dictu.*

Hotels

If you're planning on staying in Hollywood for very long, you'll probably rent or, if you can afford it, you'll buy a house. This, depending on your liquid assets, can be anything from Belle Vista (John Barrymore's grand estate) to a handyman's paradise in the Valley. If you do buy, you'll want to engage in one of Hollywood's most popular pasttimes—remodeling. Remodeling can mean anything. You can knock down the existing structure and start over from scratch, a la Mel Brooks (*Blazing Saddles*) and his wife, Anne Bancroft (*The Graduate*), in Brentwood's fashionable La Mesa Drive, or you can merely repaint the window trim. Mentioning that you're *remodeling* your house gives you a shared topic of conversation and confers a certain status—namely, that you can afford it. You don't have to go into detail. Merely complain about the difficulty of finding "good and reliable workmen" and *moan* about what it's costing you. Even the wealthiest Hollywoodians moan about what things cost. Should you feel really rash, ask for recommendations about architects and interior designers.

If you're staying in Hollywood for only a short time and are *not* being put up by friends, your bluffing road will be rocky. *Try* to stay with friends. It's a socially viable alternative, especially if you can manage to imply that your friends have the usual amenities—guest house, pool, and Jacuzzi. However, if you don't have friends in L.A., you don't. So stay in a hotel. But don't *ever* admit that you're staying at the Tropicana, even if you are. If you want to stay at the Bonaventure, realize that you'll be thought of as eccentric (which may be O.K. for some bluffers). The Bonaventure's acknowledged as being fabulous, but it's a long, *long* way from Where the Action Is. The pecking order of hotels, as far as movie folks are concerned, is as follows:

The Beverly Hills

A salmon pink cultural icon on the corner of Sunset and Beverly — you can't go wrong staying here. It's famous for its Polo Lounge — the most wheeling and dealing cocktail bar in town. You don't have to be a resident to drink here. "I'll meet you at the Polo Lounge" is as perennially Hollywood as "You oughta be in pictures." Like you can in any class bar, you can give your credit card to the waiter and have him run a tab. Discreetly maneuvered, this can give the impression that you're actually staying at the hotel. You eventually have to pay the piper, of course, but you'll have racked up a *lot* of bluffing points. It all depends on your priorities.

One advantage of hanging out at the Polo Lounge is that it invariably contains at least *one* international celebrity at almost any time of the day or night. If you're with someone whom you want to impress (a given for any bluffer), simply look across the room at a celebrity you recognize and smile or wave. They'll almost invariably smile or wave back because last month's publicity tour is already a blur and in *this* business, nobody wants to appear rude. Your table-mate will, of course, assume that you're intimately acquainted with said celebrity. The only problem: your tablemate will probably want to be introduced. One way out of this corner is to look knowingly in the celebrity's direction and confide, "She (he) *hates* to be disturbed when she's "taking a meeting."

Beyond the Polo Lounge is the Beverly Hills pool, one of the most power-laden, flesh-strewn spots on earth. Nubile young vixens, sunglassed and glistening with suntan oil, lounge alongside movie males who are pretending to read scripts and write memos. As in the Polo Lounge, the plug-in phones are a feature. These are whisked to your table or chaise lounge by a circumspect hotel staff while a modulated voice on the P.A. system murmurs, "Paging Ms. Mariellen Snodgrass . . . paging Ms. Snodgrass." If you're ever at the Polo Lounge, by the pool, or just lurking in the reception area, have a friend phone you. You can raise a nonchalant hand, have the phone plugged in, and say, loud enough for anyone at the surrounding tables to hear, "Oh, *hi*, Shirley," (it could be Temple, Jones, or MacLaine), or "Hi, Clint," or "Hi, Meryl" (how many other Clints and Meryls are there in this world?).

After a suitable pause, exclaim,"That's *fab*ulous. I know it'll be just *great* . . . No *prob*lem. I love you, babe. It's ter*rif*ic you're on board."

Now, you could have been talking to your roach exterminator, but all the big ears in Hollywood will assume that you're in the midst of "putting together a package." Being paged at the Beverly Hills is grade-A bluffing.

However, if credit cards are a problem, you don't

even have to be at the Beverly Hills. You can call the hotel and have yourself paged in the lounge or at poolside. Who's to know? You simply call the front desk and say, "Hi. I understand that Dwight Dibble is taking a meeting in the Polo Lounge. I need to talk with him right away. Can you call him to the phone?" And from far off you'll hear, "Paging Mr. Dibble."

Or there's an even bolder move—but it involves a calculated risk. Tell the receptionist, "This is Harrison Ford. I have to talk to Dwight Dibble right away. Can you call him to the phone? Tell him Harrison Ford is calling." And from far off you'll hear, "Mr. Dibble . . . Paging Mr. Dwight Dibble . . . Harrison Ford calling for Mr. Dibble."

To play this last game, however, one should first check with Celebrity Service and make sure that Harrison Ford (or whoever) is *not* in town. It could be *very* embarrassing if your celebrity choice is actually *in* the Polo Lounge when you call. Needless to say, you should pick a celebrity who's still alive. "Randolph Scott calling for Mr. Dwight Dibble" would be equally as embarrassing.

The other near-legendary feature of the Beverly Hills (which is designed to look like a Hollywood studio—front office and back lot) are its bungalows (really, the *only* place to have a clandestine assignation), which can set you back more than $1000 a night. But it's hard to imagine making that kind of bluffing investment in anyone—unless he's a Patrick Swayze look-alike.

The Bel-Air

Smallest of L.A.'s five-star hotels, the Bel-Air is farther out of town, but it's more rustic and a lot more romantic than the Beverly Hills. If you stay at the Bel-Air, the message is: you want to be alone or you've got a twinkle in your eye. Nowadays it's *far* more discreet than the Beverly Hills, if not quite as prestigious.

L'Ermitage

Not to be confused with the fashionable French restaurant of the same name on La Cienega, the reputation of this hotel on Burton Way has come up in recent years. Its main claim to fame are the paintings adorning the walls of its suites. Originally copies, they're now mostly *originals*, and they're by the likes of Renoir, Van Gogh, Picasso, Braque, and Miro. However, this idea of hanging originals isn't all that original. It's already been done at Le Coq d'Or in France. It's really not the sort of thing that impresses Hollywood anyway (not in a town that still venerates episodes of *Green Acres*).

The Beverly Wilshire

If the above are booked, it's no real loss of face to stay at the equally five-star but more conventional Beverly Wilshire, located where Rodeo Drive juts into Wilshire Boulevard. Handy for picking up those "little somethings" on Rodeo Drive, there's a Brentano's in one corner and a Tiffany's in another. Think of the time you'll save. Like the Beverly Hills, the Beverly Wilshire is High Profile.

The Chateau Marmont

An improbable multi-story structure lurching high above the north end of Sunset Strip, the Chateau Marmont is the traditional favorite of the music and com-

edy crowd. This could account for the addition of
stoves and refrigerators in the rooms in lieu of room
service. Clearly, the needs of itinerant musicians are
sometimes more – shall we say –"esoteric" than those of
actors. It's rumored that John Belushi partied here the
night he shot up – and out.

Restaurants

It used to be *nouvelle cuisine*. Now Mexican meets
Asian, and Southwestern meets Caribbean. Hollywood
food is *always* the newest of the new. Luckily, the traditional Hollywood eateries – Chasen's, the Bistro,
Scandia, L'Ermitage, Chianti, and their ilk – are still
flourishing, even expanding. The Bistro, for example,
has established a charming, floral Bistro Garden nearby, and Chianti has sucessfully launched its Chianti
Cucina annex. In addition, some of the newer entries –
the Palm on Santa Monica (designer food in an office
building that looks like a spa), Morton's, the exotic
L'Orangerie (modeled on Louis XIV's hothouse, for
those who remember it), Le Dome, and Michael's (the
patio is a *must* for Sunday brunch) – are the first and
foremost in pretension and trendiness. They're all
doing *quite* nicely, thank you.

These days, the really "in" place to be is Rebecca's.
It's on the West Side, in Venice, where, along with the
carnitas and chicken faijitas, the lamb tongue tacos, and
seviche (presented like sashimi), Escoffier flirts with
the enchilada. The decor is drop-dead dramatic – an
opulent, hard-edged, post-modern hip mix of oceanic
fauna and back-lit Travertine onyx, with mint green
Naugahyde booths. In one room an octopus chandelier

hangs from the ceiling, while in the other dangles a duo of 19-foot metal-scaled alligators. The place draws an endless stream of Porsches, Mercedes, and BMWs, and there's usually as many gawkers as eaters. The concept is by architect Frank Gehry and owners Rebecca and Bruce Marder, who also own the fashionable Mediterranean pizza parlor across the street, the West Beach Cafe.

Other chic chili-and-chipotle kitchens include Sabroso (Spanish for "tasty"), not far from Rebecca's, where the cactus salad is de*lici*ous, and on the downtown side, the original Sonora Cafe on Figueroa and the Border Grill on Melrose. The newest eateries are Trumps (starkly Southwestern), Angeli (on Melrose; what *isn't?*), the City (eclectic — French veal kidney, Poona pancakes — you get the idea), the Cha-Cha-Cha (a Caribbean hot spot), and the Mocambo (a Cuban treat for hungry mouths). *Caramba!*

But, anyway, back to Rebecca's. One of her specials is described as follows: "Baby red snapper fried with ancho chilies and sliced garlic in anchiote oil, served with tortillas, steamed spinach, and red potatoes, along with a variety of salsas and grilled rabo onions." *Mercy!* That's a mouthful — not just to eat but to remember — and there might be any number of specials available, just as lavishly described. Therefore, *always* ask what the specials are when you're introduced to "Kean," your waitperson (or "waitron," an acceptable, nonsexist term), who's likely to be an actorperson rather than a genuine food service employee. And remember, he's *not* just waiting tables; he's giving an audition.

Kean and his kind, however, are just the bit players in the restaurant scene. The prominent power wielders are the maitre d's, who, like presidential secretaries, control access to (1) just any old table, (2) an attractive table, or (3) the most prominent table in the house (the Power Table). Maitre d's have been known to parlay their positions into *lots* of cold, hard cash on any given evening.

The *real* stars of the Hollywood restaurant scene are the chefs, and the cream of the current culinary crop is Wolfgang Puck. Formerly the savior of Ma Maison, he and his wife own Spago, a nouvelle pizza and pasta restaurant on Horn, and the opulent Chinois on Main. Chinois grossed about $2.3 million in its first year of operation (a coup akin to Linda Hunt's winning an Oscar for her first film).

Other star chefs include Roy Yamaguchi at his classy 385 North (La Cienega) and, more modestly but equally as talented, Tommy Tang at his restaurant of the same name; Tom is the undisputed master of Thai food. Having a star chef come over to your table and greet you is almost as impressive as knowing Arsenio Hall or playing doubles with Merv Griffin.

Needless to say, such restaurants seek to outdo their rivals with elegance, ambiance, and the innovativeness of their cuisine. Perhaps because Hollywood is HOLLY-WOOD, restaurant design has become a grand extension of a movie set, which, when you think about it, is probably in itself welcoming to the movie crowd. The restaurants that we've mentioned are all *tres* expensive. As a bluffer, consider yourself forewarned. (A $20 bill placed in the right hands might get you a half-dozen packages of matches with the restaurant's name emblazoned upon them, which could serve your bluffing purposes quite well.)

Not surprisingly, because of their ability to command salaries of millions per picture, movie stars and other celebs are often the silent (and not-so-silent) partners in many of L.A.'s fashionable restaurants. Hampton's, for instance, a rustic and congenial hamburger house on Highland (another is on Burbank's Riverside Drive), is owned by Paul Newman (what sort of salad dressing do you suppose is served?). Dudley Moore has a piece of the action at 72 Market Street in Venice, as does Tony Bill (*The Sting*), who can often be found there tickling the ivories and amusing the patrons.

One thing you should be aware of when dining out in Hollywood: all decent restaurants, whether or not they have their own parking lot, offer valet parking. Young men and women (aspiring, wanna-be actors), dressed in spiffy uniforms, will greet you outside the restaurant and give you a ticket in exchange for your car keys. They'll park your car while you sweep elegantly inside toward your table. When your car's returned, you'll pay somewhere between $2 and $5. It can be even steeper. But if you're worried about the cost of valet parking, you really shouldn't be eating out anyway. Top drawer bluffing in Hollywood is *not* inexpensive.

Automobiles

Americans from coast to coast have an ongoing love affair with their cars. In Hollywood, however, people have so much *more* to love. The price tag on any of the Porsches or Mercedes in a restaurant parking lot represents what most Midwesterners make in a year. Strangely enough, Hollywood natives are eager to lend you their cars. They'd be far more likely to lend you their car than a book. Of course, that could be because people in Hollywood are much more likely to own cars than books.

No other city on earth is more dominated by cars than L.A. They come in all shapes and sizes – from the smallest beat-up, sub-compact (those unsafe-at-any-speed Corvairs), to exotic imports, to mag-wheeled dune buggies. For around $300 an hour, you can hire a forty-foot-long stretch limo, complete with chauffeur, mink-lined seats, TV, video, bar, Jacuzzi, and an optionally topless male or female "escort." Bluffers take note, tasteful understatement doesn't exist in Hollywood. Big, expensive, garish cars are the only thing that can upstage the Stars.

Inevitably, in status-conscious Hollywood, the car you drive reflects the kind of person you are, much more so than where you live, because people never have to see your tacky, roach-infested apartment. Bluffers never *ever* invite people over. You meet them at, say, the aforementioned Polo Lounge. Everyone will see your car and assume you're successful. That's why even struggling young actors with little more than a change of Levis and a pair of Ray-Bans will manage to drive something impressive – if not expensive, at least kicky.

You can buy, lease, or rent a car in L.A. of whatever make or style you can afford. It's a big business here, and it pays to shop around. But *remember*, if you want to impress (which really *is* the point, after all), you can rent a high-profile car for a day, an evening, or an hour, return it as soon as the impressing is done, and head home in your Rent-a-Wreck.

One more thing. When you first arrive in L.A., it's best to carry a compass. Los Angelenos do *not* give directions like normal people do: "Go straight ahead at the lights, turn right, then take the second left." In contrast, Los Angelenos tell you to "go south on La Cienega, then west on Wilshire . . ." If you haven't a clue which direction you're facing, this can be confusing. Remember too that Hollywood natives have a great propensity for giving distances in time rather than miles. "How far is it to MGM?" About 20 minutes.

The Arts

In a town where a-r-t means an apple-raisin-tuna salad, *Art* is a fringe pursuit indulged in *only* by the sucessful and rich, who understand that a small Picasso or Renoir is a wonderful hedge against inflation and also an elegant and obvious status symbol. Although it's fashionable to *collect* art, it's considered showy to know *too* much about it—beyond its dollar value.

L.A. has lots of rich, culture-crazed philanthropists lavishing great sums on galleries and collections, and the jewel in the crown of L.A. art galleries is undoubtedly the J. Paul Getty Museum, overlooking the Pacific Coast Highway as you enter Malibu. The museum itself is an improbable white marble replica of the Villa dei Papiri at Herculaneum, the original of which was destroyed in A.D. 79, when Vesuvius torched Pompeii.

Set in formal gardens, the Getty houses three major collections—Greek and Roman antiquities, Western European paintings, and French decorative arts. The Getty's acquisitions, which include Dutch master Jan

Steen's *The Drawing Master* and Cezanne's *Nature Morte*, are funded by a $2.2 *billion* trust, a private foundation that (because of tax laws) *must* spend at least $92.4 million each year. The Getty Trust is therefore *the* major player in the international art world, its budget dwarfing New York's Metropolitan Museum of Art's ($30 million per annum), Chicago's Art Institute's ($36 million) and even the Rockefeller Foundation's.

Critics have sometimes looked down their noses at the quality of the Getty's purchases, sneering that the Getty helped inflate the prices of the international art market beyond the competitive resources of such poor relations as the Tate and the British National Gallery. The Getty says that that's sour grapes.

Meanwhile, rumors surface from time to time that the Getty collection will one day be joined with the Norton Simon art collection in Pasadena, the collection of philanthropist Norton Simon (husband of Jennifer *Duel in the Sun* Jones) to comprise one of the most important art collections in the United States – and in the world. (In a town that loves to speculate on "packages," this is a juicy "package" of gossip, indeed).

The big changes in the art world over the past few years are MOCA and MONA, neither of which is a Brazilian coffee blend. MOCA (Museum of Contemporary Art) is probably *the* most exciting thing to hit the L.A. art scene. Prestigious and impressive as the Getty, the Norton Simon, and the Huntington are, they all house "institutionalized art," meaning art that has passed the test of time (relatively speaking) and has become Art. (Anybody with an IQ in the double digits – and there's a lot of them – can figure out that a Gainsborough or a Cezanne is worth investing in).

It's a whole other ballgame with MOCA. Unlike L.A. museums that revel in the institutionalized past, MOCA houses contemporary art, and given that we know what "contemporary" means, the pertinent questions that people ask themselves before investing in the art they admire in MOCA are: "Is it any good?" and "Is it *art*?" Stars and moviemakers who can't afford to compete with Old Master Getty but are still seeking a hedge against inflation and have an odd $100 thousand to throw around are often found in MOCA. Likewise, working artists have flocked into the downtown vicinity of MOCA, trailing realtors and chichi restaurants in their wake.

Leaving MOCA and moving on to MONA, be aware, first of all, that we're talking about the Museum of *Neon* Art. The neon pieces here are no mere "Eat at Joe's," although old signs are very much in vogue. The museum features large, decorative neon scultures, as well as designs and drawings in neon. Now anyone (you too) can have their name in lights.

There are lots of theaters and music centers in L.A., but for everything from Paganini to Pop, the favorite place to go in summer is the open-air Hollywood Bowl—home of the Los Angeles Philharmonic. A natural phenomenon (these are rare in Hollywood, geographically or otherwise), the Bowl provides the backdrop for "Under the Boardwalk," one of the songs that Bette Midler croons in *Beaches*. The complex also contains a Hollywood Museum, where you can see the barn in which the first Western was made. Relocated from its former site at Paramount, the museum is now a California State Historical Monument.

HOLLYWOOD:
MOVIES AND TV

Whenever someone says that a movie has "universal appeal," what they're really saying is that it could be about *themselves*. Not surprisingly, Hollywood movies reflect Hollywood concerns—that is,

Disaster Movies—Hollywood is prone to all kinds of natural disasters—from brush fires to flooding, from mud slides to (of course) earthquakes.

Frankenstein Movies—The plastic surgeon gets it all wrong.

Airplane Movies—Everyone here flies a lot, and, as it turns out, we have every reason to be afraid.

Dracula Movies—Aging movie exec lusts after young starlet and gets a stake through his heart—a parable for his wife finding out, divorcing him, and taking half of everything.

Treasure Hunt/Robbery Movies—When they get away with it, we've got the Hollywood version of the American Dream: Life, Liberty, and the Pursuit of Big Bucks.

Age-Can-Be-Licked Movies—Like *Cocoon*. Every aging star's secret wish.

Haunted House Movies—In security-paranoid Hollywood, some crazy has by-passed your alarm system

and is about to rip you off, or worse. Did you see
Alien? You thought it was just a space monster
movie? Huh-uh. It was about Charlie Manson.

Comic Book Movies—*Dick Tracy, Batman,* and *Popeye.*
In Hollywood, this is literature.

Beat-the-System Movies (male)—You finally become
head of a corporation and answer to *nobody.*

Beat-the-System Movies (female)—You become
Sherry Lansing (head of Fox).

Divorce Movies—*Kramer vs. Kramer, Heartburn.*
Enough said.

Buddy Movies—Once upon a time (pre-Hollywood),
we knew what it was to have friends we could trust.

Westerns—These used to be called Horse Operas.
Now, all of the obligatory shooting and chasing takes
place in and around cars. The supermarket or studio
parking lot is the hitching post of the Last Chance
Saloon. Valet parking is the stables where the old guy
with a limp used to say, "It's 10 cents for a rub-down,
water, and feed." You say, "Take good care of her" and
saunter in to do battle with a surly maitre d'.

Movies

Movies are an illusion, a complete con from start to
finish. The eye is deceived. It does *not* see a "progress-
ing" event. Instead, it sees a series of still photographic
images. In addition, stunt men and women stand in
for the real stars during the dangerous bits, night shots
are done during the day, one of the canyons around

Hollywood doubles for the Old West, and another galaxy far, far away turns out to be Universal's back lot. Making movies is Big Time Bluffing. It's what Hollywood does for a living. Just remember that Appearance and Reality get a little confusing out here. And to complicate matters further, remember that in Hollywood, you shouldn't ever confuse Movies with Films (with a capital 'F') or, God forbid, with Cinema (capital 'C').

To speak of Films and Cinema is to speak the language of history and aesthetics—which comes with a smattering of French. These terms are reserved for pictures made "abroad" or long ago, and often the actors who made them are dead. This mind-set assumes that Films (especially silent, black-and-white, and foreign films) are jam-packed with critical and artistic "meaning." Required reading includes magazines like *Sight and Sound* and *Cahiers du Cinema*. Everyone pays lip service to how *grand* (and *classic*) these films are (were), but in Hollywood today, especially since the death of Orson Welles, the potential for large grosses wins out over art *every* time.

"Movies" are another thing altogether. Movies are about what is happening *now*, about entertainment and about money—that is, movies are pictures currently in release, projects in development, stars, marquee values and bankability, budgets, box-office trends, and distribution grosses. Required bluffer reading are trade papers like *Variety* and the *Hollywood Reporter*. To see a Movie, you go to "screenings." True dyed-in-the-glitz Hollywoodians thrill to rumors about what Dustin or Meryl is going to do next. They gossip about the "above the line" on *Ishtar,* look down their noses at *Dangerous*

Liaisons's chances of "breaking even," and they always, *always* have their *own* projects.

In other words, Hollywood is more about *Rambo* than it is about *Jules et Jim*, and its citizenry are only too aware that in the movies, "art" is only incidental (sometimes even accidental). The true business of Movies is Business. Indeed, in Hollywood to be in the Movies is referred to as being "in the business" (as opposed to "being in the art form"). There's an old adage that states: in Hollywood, the real art form is not the picture but the deal.

A word of explanation on "above the line." This term refers to the salaries of the writer, the producer, the director, and the Stars—particularly when the combination adds up to more than the cost of the rest of the picture. It's not an everyday occurrence, but Stars *are* expensive—and not just in terms of their above-the-line salaries or down-the-line profits. To budget for a Star, you immediately add 30 percent for the Star's demands—for example,

Perks—Emperor-sized waterbeds on Sahara locations; Meryl demands a studio for her sculptor husband; Joe Piscopo has to have a personal weight trainer.

Entourages—Some Stars whine to have the *entire staff* of Vidal Sassoon do their make-up and hair.

Tantrums—"I can't *work* under these conditions" or "Get my agent on the phone. He knows I'm *never* shot from this side."

It all adds up. And you know what? For a real Star, it's worth it. Dustin Hoffman may be a notorious, demanding crank on the set, but he's a crank that directors are dying to cast in their next movie.

Movie History

Movies began in 1824 when Englishman Peter Roget discovered an aspect of perceptual behavior called "persistence of vision." Our eye/brain computer needs a little "memory time" to process the information sifting into it. After this discovery, it was only a "short take" (movie-speak for "it wasn't long") before scientists and illustrators realized that because of "persistence of vision," a series of frames could be contrived ("frozen moments of time," in the words of the pompous director in *Hooper*, supposedly modeled on Peter Bogdanovich). And after these "moments" were "contrived," they could be presented in sequence. The result was the zoetrope, or the "wheel-of-life spinning drum" (before it became the name of Francis Ford Coppola's production company). This illustrated frame-by-frame process is still the basis of Disney cartoons.

In 1887, Eadweard Muybridge, another Englishman, succeeded in analyzing motion with a camera (to settle a bet for California railway magnate Leland Stanford). He proved that a horse's hooves at full gallop *all* left the ground at some point. Muybridge used 24 cameras attached to trip wires. Later, he invented a form of projector which ran his pictures as an apparition of moving reality.

But it was an American genius, Thomas Alva Edison, who invented (along with a thousand or more other gadgets) the Kinetoscope, a combined movie camera and projector, with edge perforations to move the film through.

The next breakthrough was the perfection of the modern type of projector by Thomas Armat. His machine was first shown publicly at the Cotton States exhibition in Atlanta in 1895. It displayed Edison Kinetoscope pictures. It was subsequently known as the Vitascope. A year later, the first commercial showing of a movie took place in a New York music hall, and the history of motion pictures began.

The earliest movies were little more than brief scenes of real life, and the first movie theaters, once the showmen had moved out of the converted storerooms they started in, were known as nickelodeons—it cost a nickel to see the movies. Before long, these early moviemakers realized the narrative possibilities of their new medium, and in 1903, the tremendously influential *Great Train Robbery* was made by Edwin S. Porter. Employing "editing" (a brand-new term), it displayed a heightened sense of story, action, and drama and was the longest-running film of its day—a full 11 minutes.

These movie pioneers used either Edison equipment or equipment utilizing Edison's inventions, which he had patented. The moviemakers, however, were generally disinclined to pay the required license fees, so various Edison patent trusts were formed to locate and hound production companies for patent infringement. Shooting was often interrupted by the imminent arrival of the patent trust agents, and the filmmakers would scatter as fast as Mississippi moonshiners, carrying away as much of their precious equipment as they could. It's often said that the reason why early filmmakers went to Hollywood was the weather—endless days of sunshine, good light (pre-smog days), and no interruptions from the rain. More pressing reasons included the fact that southern California was a long way from Edison's New York patent trusts and close to Mexico. Should a moviemaker suspect that he was likely to be busted—not an infrequent occurrence—he could make a run for the border.

The first production company to locate in Hollywood was David Horsley's Nestor Film Company (1911), which leased a site on the northwest corner of Sunset and Gower. Fifteen other movie companies were established in the neighborhood by the end of the year, with more on the way, many of them appearing or disappearing overnight, all churning out "one- and two-reelers" for 10-cent theaters and an audience that was estimated to be about 10 million.

In 1913, Cecil B. De Mille, Jesse Lasky, and Samuel Goldwyn combined their know-how to produce *The Squaw Man* in the now-famous barn just a block from Hollywood and Vine. This Western was the first major movie produced in Hollywood, and it was an enormous hit. In 1915, D. W. Griffith made the classic *Birth of a Nation.* The movies (and Hollywood) were here to stay.

After the first few hectic years, the movie business settled down into an established pattern whose legacy is still with us today. In general, it was dominated by seven studios—the Big 5 (MGM, RKO, Fox, Warner, and Paramount) and the Little 2 (Universal and Columbia). Each of the separate studios had its own geographical area (land on which their movies were made), production financing, distribution, networks, and exhibition chains (movie houses).

In the moviemaking heydays of the 20s and 30s, sound was introduced, and Al Jolson announced in *The Jazz Singer,* "You ain't heard nothing yet, folks!" (a bluffer's line that was unmatched until Dirty Harry snarled, "Go ahead, make my day"). All the studios turned out hundreds of pictures every year, and they all had a stable of writers, producers, directors, carpenters, location managers, publicists – you name it – and, of course, actors and Stars (note the distinction), all under contract as full-time employees.

Circumstances have changed. Box-office revenues declined drastically with the advent of television in the late 40s. Almost simultaneously, the studios were hit with a series of antitrust lawsuits, which took away their chains of movie houses. Since the 50s, movie studios have been on a financial rollercoaster downward. RKO disappeared, bought out by Desilu (of *I Love Lucy* fame). In a scramble to remain solvent, some of the other studios sold off part of their real estate (like Fox) or *everything* (like Columbia). The rest bit the bullet, joined the enemy, and went into television production. Now they're owned, for the most part, by humongous, multinational conglomerates.

Today, Universal is Hollywood's largest and busiest studio, spread over 420 acres on the northern, valley side of the Hollywood Hills, known modestly as Universal City. How busy is it? It's so busy that the Sheraton Hotel chain has built a hotel within a stone's throw of it to house all of the itinerants generated.

One of Universal's solutions during its financial troubles was to launch the Universal Studios tour. The tour attracts 3.5 million-plus visitors a year at between $10 and $15 a head. Throw in the fast food and merchandising concessions, and you can safely say that the gross from the tour could pay the light bill for a couple of months.

The tour includes Western sets, Mexican villages, fake New York tenement buildings, and a glimpse of Norman Bates' *Psycho* house. There's also fake rock-slides and a fake collapsing bridge, a demonstration of how Moses (Cecil B. De Mille, actually) parted the Red Sea in the 1956 *Ten Commandments* (it's actually footage of two waterfalls), and explanations of other special effects—for example, you get to see how Superman flies. Real uptown stuff. You can also stroll through the dressing rooms of famous Stars (like the late Lucille Ball), and there's live Western stunts and animal shows (whoop-de-do)—and the King Kong attraction, featuring the World's Largest Animated Figure (30 feet high), housed in a 26,000 square-foot sound stage. Take the tour for Kong alone. He menaces you on the tour tram in a recreation of the famous train scene from the movie. You'll *love* it. Afterwards, be blasé about it. Shrug and say, "Well, we had to take the *kids*." Or say, "If you've seen one ape,' you've seen 'em all."

Television

If you throw in the cable and satellite suppliers, along with the syndication companies and networks, there are over 40 TV channels available in Hollywood—24 hours, day and night. This is tele-heaven for blocked writers, tele-addicts, and insomniacs, who want to stay in bed and play with their remotes.

Aside from the Hollywood TV menu being bigger, it's also more varied. The cable and satellite subscription channels, like "Z" (pronounced "Zee") and HBO (Home Box Office), offer hit movies almost before they're in the theaters. There's also an after-hours adult

movie channel (read *X-rated*). You can also watch ethnic channels – Mexican soap operas, the most blatant in the world, and Japanese soap operas, the most bloodcurdling in the world.

The sheer amount of television in Hollywood is prodigious. But bluffers should know that despite the fact that, worldwide, more people watch American TV than see American "movies," in status-conscious Hollywood, movies are steak and television is hamburger. Movies are sushi, television is bait. When a former Star takes a role in a soap opera, it's tantamount to a concession that she's (or he's) no longer *bankable* on the big screen. For all her money and success, Joan Collins knew that her movie career was over once she signed her contract for *Dynasty.* In this town, it's the Oscars, not the Emmys that *really* count.

THE HOLLYWOOD
STATE OF MIND

High Anxiety

In their heart of hearts, most movie stars are a worried lot. They may have money, glamour, and fame, but are they happy? You bet your sweet bippy they are. However, they know that they're popular at the whim of the public and that the public can be *very* fickle. They worry about receding hairlines and thickening waistlines (Jane Fonda has put this latter anxiety to work, creating a video exercise gold mine). They worry if their agent doesn't send a limo to meet them at the airport. They worry about the scripts that they're asked to read: are they right for *me*? Who read this before me? (Bogart, for example, worried that he never got any good lines; few have received so many.) They worry about appearing with animals (Rex Harrison tells horrific tales about the filming of *Dr. Doolittle*), and they worry about appearing with children (*Three Men and a Baby*, however, showed off Tom Selleck, Ted Danson, and Steve Guttenberg to their best advantage). They worry that they're not as tall as people imagine them to be (Alan Ladd had to stand on a box to play love scenes with Sophia Loren), and they worry that the most popular actor in 1933 was Mickey Mouse. But most of all, they worry about when the public is going to stop liking them—and what if their next film is a flop and the phone stops ringing.

They *should* worry. It *can* happen. Warren Beatty hasn't made a phenomenally successful film since *Reds*. It's said that Dustin Hoffman demanded that the part of the younger brother in *Rain Man* be rewritten, changing the age from 38 to 28 so that Tom Cruise (with his youthful *Top Gun* audience in tow) could play the part. One more *Ishtar* for either Hoffman or Beatty, and they'll be doing Preparation H or Depend commercials.

Money Matters

The basic elements of moviemaking are finance, production, distribution, and exhibition. The last three are phases—like sex, marriage, and children—but Finance is Life itself.

The average Hollywood movie today costs at least $15 million (or about half of the yearly take from the Universal Studio tours). This is the *negative cost*—that is, how much it costs to produce the edited, dubbed, and scored negative of the movie from which the *positives* (or prints) are struck.

Depending on the length of a picture, prints average out at about $2000 each. Should you, as a movie mogul, want your film to open across the country in a thousand theaters on the same holiday weekend (*Rambo LXIX*/Fourth of July, *Ghostbusters VIII*/ Christmas, you get the idea), you'll need at least 1000 prints. That's another couple of million right there. Then, naturally, you want your prints to actually arrive in time ("distribution"). And you'll want people to have heard of your movie before it hits town, so you'll have taken out ads in newspapers, or run an eye-catching TV commercial ("promotion and advertising"). Meanwhile, all this money is costing you money ("interest"). And you *also* have to maintain a staff of people and facilities to see that all of this is being done properly ("overhead").

Conventional wisdom maintains that just for a movie to "break even," it needs to gross virtually 3 times its "negative cost." This is known as "the multiple," the sacred formula on which so many deals are cut, fortunes made and lost, and studios built or buried.

America contains at least 60 percent of the world market for movies. Its "core audience"—those who go to the movies more than once a year (most of them are between the ages of 14 and 25)—is about 14 million. The current average ticket price is about $3.60. If all 14 million go to see your $15 million movie, the box office take will be $50.4 million. So, has the movie earned itself $5.4 million clear? Not quite. The box-office pie still has to be sliced up.

The "exhibitor" (theater owner or chain) takes his slice and pays his mortgages, managers, projectionists, cleaners, and ushers—not to mention himself. This is money "off the top."

All kinds of wheeling and dealing go on between the distributor and an exhibitor to establish how *much* is taken "off the top." What they're trying to establish is "the split"—90/10 or 80/20, or whatever—and sometimes, an exhibitor may indulge in a little extra-curricular "skimming." In any event, it's the amount that's returned to the distributor that's important, for this is known as the "distributor's gross"—and this is the basic reality (if there is such a thing as "reality" in Hollywood) of moviemaking.

Distributors have often been known to employ creative (wink, wink) accounting. This can keep even a financially successful picture ever so *slightly* in the red and avoid paying the actors who might be "profit participants" (whose contracts stipulate a "piece of the action" in lieu of money up front). The further away from gross you are, the more looking at profits resembles looking through the wrong end of a telescope.

For producers, there are other ways of finagling the profits. If they can get a heaven-sent script by, say, Bill (*Butch Cassidy*) Goldman and entice Michael Douglas and Kathleen Turner to play in it with Norman ("Moonstruck") Jewison directing, you'll have what is known as a "package." This is the consumate Hollywood Dream. While fending off the studios who want this "package" for worldwide distribution so badly that they are willing to throw in a Triple-PSL (Permanent Personalized Parking Space for Life), you'll travel all over the globe obtaining terrific "distribution deals" (pre-sales and guarantees). Think of it. Separate "distribution deals" in every separate distribution area in the world — U.S., Europe, Japan (very big, Japan), Australia, and so forth.

Should you be the one in a million who can put together this kind of deal, it's possible to raise more money than the picture will cost to shoot before you've even started shooting. Thus, you're already in the black even if your picture turns out lousy. But if it's a smash, you'll be hip deep in happy dust.

It's brutally hard work, taxing on the nerves, and expensive. But it's *not* crazy. A lot of pictures get made this way, and it's why the De Laurentiises and the Spiegels of this world have stayed ahead of the game. Great moviemakers or great showmen or great salesmen or great bluffers—in Hollywood, it's all the same. It's also the reason—when someone comes up with a winning formula—that they keep squeezing the goose that lays the golden eggs. In the lingo of the business, we're talking "spin-offs"—that is, sequels (the story continues ad nauseam: *Karate Kid XVI*, *Police Academy XIX*, and so forth), prequels (the story *before* the story: *Butch Cassidy and the Sundance Kid—The Early Years.*), and remakes (same story, different cast: *King Kong, A Star Is Born,* and *Lost Horizon*).

Sometimes a movie is a smash hit and nobody understands why. It doesn't have a major star, the story appealed to the wrong age group, it was made only as a tax write-off (or so that the director's toy boy could have a third lead role). This kind of hit is known as a "non-recurring phenomenon," which is a pseudo accounting term for "We have no idea, so shut up and take the money."

WHO'S WHO IN HOLLYWOOD

Studio Heads

Nowadays they're referred to (with a straight face) as the "heads of production," or the "heads of creative affairs." They're the studio bosses. They may not actually *own* the studio (like in the old days), but they're still the people with Power. They're the people who ultimately decide *which* stories will be developed, *which* scripts will be promoted, *which* directors and stars are bankable, *which* packages are financeable, and *which* pictures get made. They're the people who sign the checks. Find out their names and be nice to them.

Independent Producers

The role once played by the oldtime moguls is now played by "independent producers." These folks come packaged in all shapes and sizes and in expensive forms of transportation. Jerry Bruckheimer (*Beverly Hills Cop, I* and *II*) is known for his fleet of black cars (*not* Chevys). They're the daring souls who put together dazzling packages. Michael Douglas spent some time producing before he made the leap to screen popularity. Jon Peters traded up to producing from teasing the tresses of the rich and well connected. Steven

Spielberg, his reputation established as a director, lends his name to projects as their "executive producer" in order to encourage box-office success.

In a more exclusive club than producers are those who take on more than one task in the production – that is, producer-director, writer-producer, or even writer-actor. The alert bluffer will pick up on what a handy ploy this is for doubling your salary. The only possible drawback is that it *does* require some knowledge of what you're doing – things like acting or writing or, say, directing a movie. Not insurmountable, but recommended for advanced bluffers only.

Ordinary bluffers might want to start by hinting that they're producers. Should someone actually ask what you've done, here's a list of some of the things that producers do:

(1) find the basic story, or "property"– the idea, play, or book on which the movie is based,
(2) attract other "creative elements," such as the director and the stars of the project,
(3) make the deals for production, finance, and distribution, and
(4) supposedly oversee how the production money is spent during shooting, editing, and so forth.

Obviously, each of these phases involves a delicate process of power brokering, diplomacy, and negotiation. In a way, directors can be said to *make* movies, but it's the producer who makes moviemaking *happen*.

It's important to note that no one ever says that they're "turning to independent production." In the business, this is a euphemism for "I've been fired." It usually applies to studio production executives who've been axed and are pensioned off with some "production deal," often worthless and usually in lieu of some more tangible compensation they might be entitled to — like cash.

Production Managers

While egos run rampant on the set and in the plush offices of the deal-makers, it's the production manager's job to actually get the movie made. Production managers are the people who actually draw up the shooting schedules and budgets and monitor the expenditures before, during, and after shooting — night and day. While the producers are wining and dining their stars in the swankest restaurants (on their expense accounts, of course), the production manager is working into the wee hours, arranging early morning calls, transportation, and what-to-do if tomorrow's shoot is wiped out by a monsoon. If there's a problem — any problem at all — it's up to the production manager to sort it out. Production managers are the nuts and bolts of moviemaking. No movie can be made without them.

Agents

The ten percenters. The biggest agencies in town are ICM, CAA, and William Morris. Top agents like Sue Mengers, Stan Kamen, and Swifty Lazaar, wield *enormous* power. They've been around for a long time, but even relative newcomers like Sandy Gallin are given their due in a competitive town like this one. Unlike studio bosses who frequently play executive musical chairs, agents tend to stick with one agency. They leave *only* to become producers, to form their own agencies (when they realize that they aren't going to become the top gun of the agency that they are with), or to become studio bosses themselves.

Top agents have working and personal relationships with *everyone* who is *anyone* in town. They can usually reach whomever they like — studio bosses and stars — with a single call ("Hi, babe, luv ya! Gotta run, sweetheart, I've got the Pope on line 2. It's been *real*"). They've done some Big Favors over the years, knowing that someday it'll be Payback Time, and they know where *all* the bodies are buried. Agents are the ones who make the deals — even though, in their gut of guts, they know that they're merely the middle men (or women) of the business.

Agents' clients never think that they're doing *quite enough* for them, and regardless of how much they do *do,* their clients will eventually leave them for another agency. Being constantly dumped for someone else may have contributed to the oft-heard remark "colder than an agent's heart." Power may be a poor substitute for love, but there's no denying that it pays better and gets one nicer tables in the restaurants that count. This is the trade-off for agents.

Having an agent is a considerable adornment in Hollywood. It means that someone is taking you seriously, that you're On Your Way. Having a top agent is like having a charge account at Giorgio's.

Getting an agent, however, is the tough part. When you really need one, when you're new in town and struggling, nobody with any Star Power is interested. When you've clearly started your climb, every agent in town will want a piece of your action. Agents are perennially like Samuel Johnson's sometime-patron Lord Chesterfield, to whom he wrote, "Is not a patron, my lord, one who looks with unconcern on a man struggling for his life in the water, and when he has reached ground, encumbers him with help?"

Stars

Everybody in Hollywood knows that it's really the *movie* that's the star—only they don't know *which* movie far enough in advance. Even sequels and remakes can bomb (*Cocoon II* played for about five minutes in theaters). Movies are always unreliable; they have no track record. You have no idea what the response will be until the sneak previews, and you can be wrong even then. Movies have played well in preview and still died at the box-office.

Writers, directors and, above all, that most gilded, famous and rich group—the Movie Stars themselves—*do* have track records. And since backing a picture is a lot like backing a horse, studio execs study the number of Stars that go to make up the "package." Stars can't guarantee that a horse will win, but they do get the horse out of the gate, shorten the odds, and, if the result is a disaster, they can help the exec save some face in the end ("We're talking Darryl Hannah—how could *I* know nobody would like her as a cave woman?").

Burt Reynolds as Bandit; Clint Eastwood as Dirty Harry; Sylvester Stallone as Rocky or Rambo; Harrison Ford as Indiana Jones—these are the most consistently bankable stars. Redford (when he isn't directing), Newman, Nicholson, Brando (if you can entice him off his island), Hoffman, and De Niro are right up there too, and in a variety of roles. Eddie Murphy and Bill Murray are too—in any kind of comedy.

Although it's not conventional Hollywood wisdom to bankroll a picture on a woman, Barbra Streisand in a musical (and occasionally a serious picture like *Nuts*) is a Star; so is Goldie Hawn in a wacky comedy. Meryl Streep could read the Yellow Pages aloud (in a variety of accents) and still be a bankable Star.

Every Star has his or her Disappointments. Nobody wanted to see Sylvester Stallone as a union leader in *F.I.S.T.* or Clint Eastwood in *Bronco Billy,* or Streisand in *Yentl,* or Bill Murray in *The Razor's Edge,* but these were projects that were obviously close to their hearts. However, the presence of a Star in a picture—any picture—guarantees that exhibitors will book it (before anyone's even seen it) and that a large, initial audience will turn out just from fan loyalty and curiosity. This is what enables Stars to get their fabulous salaries and percentages. They get projects off the ground. They ensure that their movies open. Stars are like 30-foot gorillas, and you know what they say: Where does a 30-foot gorilla sleep? Anywhere it wants to.

In Hollywood, the aura of stardom lingers longer than the reality, the way ex-presidents are still called "Mr. President." Tony Curtis remains a semi-Star. But can he carry a picture? As a limited performer, probably. As the father of Jamie Lee Curtis, Ohhh, maybe. But are the Hollywood Powers That Be going to beat a path to his door? He shouldn't hold his breath. Do they think a Tony Curtis picture will make the distribution people drool with anticipation? No way. And the same goes for, say, Doris Day, Glenn Ford, and a host of other Names who will never exactly be Has Beens in this town. They aren't washed up, either, but they're over the hill as far as being a cog in the megabucks machinery.

Once a Star's usefulness (read *moneymaking ability*) is deemed spent, Hollywood becomes a very pragmatic, therefore a very cruel, town. But, on the other hand, surprising comebacks *do* take place. Who would have figured George Burns to make the comeback that he pulled off in his 80s? And why, on the basis of *Oh, God!* and *The Sunshine Boys,* was he was allowed to turn out several "dogs" in a row (*18 Again,* for instance).

Directors

Some directors are Stars — Steven Spielberg being several of them. Woody Allen is; Hitchcock was; Sidney (*Out of Africa, Tootsie*) Pollack probably is; Robert Redford might be.

Directors are the people who take the script and tell the cameramen how to shoot the movie. They're significantly involved in every major creative aspect. They interpret the scenes, guide and motivate their actors, decide on the lighting, have the last word on camera angles, say "ACTION," "CUT," and "PRINT," monitor the dailies ("rushes"), and supervise all post-production editing, dubbing, scoring, and so on. If producers can be compared to field marshals, directors are the generals who fight the battle.

In the old days, directors were just contract employees like everyone else. But in recent years their status has been considerably enhanced. The French

New Wave directors were the most conscientious at doing this, calling themselves the *auteurs* (authors) of their movies rather than the more traditional *realisateurs* (directors). This was a considerable sock in the eye for the screenwriters, who had always thought that *they* were the authors—particularly if they had come up with an original script and hadn't merely rewritten one of the rewrites or adaptations that someone else had written or rewritten. But it's long been a standard practice to offer legitimate authors (novelists and playwrights) a *lot* of money to produce less than their best effort. It's also standard practice for the writer to complain bitterly about this situation—but not too loudly, if the money is good.

Louis Malle can get away with calling himself an *auteur,* but remember that he's annexed himself to Hollywood by marrying Candice Bergen. Perhaps the only American director who is truly an *auteur* is Woody Allen. But he lives and works in New York. Barry Levinson has shown *auteur* potential with his highly personalized movies (*Diner, Tin Men*) and has filled the gap that was left by self-acclaimed *auteur* and inflated egoist Peter Bogdanovich.

Writers

Writers don't rate very highly on the Hollywood totem pole. Like critics, *everybody* thinks they can write—from the kid in the mail room to the producer's gardener. They can be illiterate and *still* think they could have written a better script. Production executives don't even bother to read scripts. They have readers do it for them. Then, if the reader likes it, the exec will have an assistant read it for him. Maybe the exec will read a synopsis. Usually, though, all they'll want is to hear the "jingle" (the Cliff Notes version in ten words or less).

There's an old gag line about a dumb starlet. How dumb was she? She was so dumb that she went to bed with a scriptwriter.

And that's Hollywood.